PRAYING THE PSALMS

Thomas Merton
PRAYING
THE PSALMS

The Liturgical Press
Collegeville, Minnesota

Cover photo: Courtesy of Gethsemani Archives, Abbey of
            Gethsemani, Trappist, Kentucky
Cover design: Cathleen Casey

Quotations from the psalms in this booklet are taken from *The
Psalms, A Prayer Book,* courtesy of Benziger Brothers, Inc., New
York. The numbering of the Psalms follows that of the Vulgate and
the Septuagint (Greek) Bible.

Nihil obstat: John Eidenschink, O.S.B., J.C.D., *Censor
deputatus. Imprimatur:* ✠Peter W. Bartholome, D.D., Bishop of
St. Cloud. May 25, 1955.

PRAYING THE PSALMS

Why has the Church always considered the Psalms her most perfect book of prayer? Why do the Psalms go to make up the greater part of the Office recited by her priests and religious? Why, too, should the Christian layman turn to the Psalms and make use of them in his own prayer to God?

Does the Church love the Psalms merely because they are ancient, venerable religious poems? Merely out of conservative refusal to change? Or does she use them because she has been commanded to do so by God? Does she sing them merely because they are the revealed word of God?

The Church indeed likes what is old, not because it is old but rather because it is "young." In the Psalms, we drink divine praise at its pure and stainless source, in all its primitive sincerity and perfection. We return to the youthful strength and directness with which the ancient psalmists voiced their adoration of the God of Israel. Their adoration was intensified by the ineffable accents of new discovery: for the Psalms are the songs of men who *knew who God was.* If we are to pray well, we too must discover the Lord to whom we speak, and if we use the Psalms in our prayer we will stand a better chance of sharing in the discovery which lies hidden in their words for all generations. For God has willed to make Himself known to us in the mystery of the Psalms.

The Psalms are not only the revealed word of God, not only the words which God Himself has indicated to be those which He likes to hear from us. The Church does not love the Psalter merely because it is imposed on her from without, by a divine command. The Psalter is too close to the sources of her own life. The Psalms are not only the songs of prophets inspired by God, they are the songs of the whole Church, the very expression of her deepest inner life. The words and thoughts of the Psalms spring not only from the unsearchable depths of God, but also from the inmost heart of the Church, and there are no songs which better express her soul, her desires, her longing, her sorrows and her joys.

The reason why the Church loves the Psalms, then, is not merely that they have been sent to her by God from His far-distant heaven, but because God has given Himself to her in them, as though in a sacrament. The Church loves to sing over and over again the songs of the old psalmists because in them she is singing of her knowledge of God, of her union with Him.

But God has given Himself to us in Christ. The Psalms are full of the Incarnate Word. Not only is David a "type" of Christ, but the whole

Psalter has always been regarded by the Church, in her liturgy, as though it were a summary and compendium of all that God has revealed. In other words the Psalms contain in themselves all the Old and New Testaments, the whole Mystery of Christ. In singing the Psalms each day, the Church is therefore singing the wedding hymn of her union with God in Christ.

To put it very plainly: the Church loves the Psalms because in them she sings of her experience of God, of her union with the Incarnate Word, of her contemplation of God in the Mystery of Christ.

She recommends the Psalms to her priests, her monks, her nuns, and even to her laypeople, in order that they may have "the mind of Christ," in order that they may develop an interior life which is truly the life of their Mother, the Church. It is by singing the Psalms, by meditating on them, loving them, using them in all the incidents of our spiritual life, that we enable ourselves to enter more deeply into that active participation in the liturgy which is the key to the deepest and truest interior life. If we really come to know and love the Psalms, we will enter into the Church's own experience of divine things. We will begin to know God as we ought. And that is why the Church believes the Psalms are the best possible way of praising God.

To praise God!

Do we know what it means to praise? To adore? To give glory?

Praise is cheap today. Everything is praised. Soap, beer, toothpaste, clothing, mouthwash, movie stars, all the latest gadgets which are supposed to make life more comfortable—everything is constantly being "praised." Praise is now so overdone that everybody is sick of it, and since everything is "praised" with the official hollow enthusiasm of the radio announcer, it turns out in the end that *nothing* is praised. Praise has become empty. Nobody really wants to use it.

Are there any superlatives left for God? They have all been wasted on foods and quack medicines. There is no word left to express our adoration of Him who alone is Holy, who alone is Lord.

So we go to Him to ask help and to get out of being punished, and to mumble that we need a better job, more money, more of the things that are praised by the advertisements. And we wonder why our prayer is so often dead—gaining its only life, borrowing its only urgency from the fact that we need these things so badly.

But we do not really think we need God. Least of all do we think we need to praise Him.

It is quite possible that our lack of interest

in the Psalms conceals a secret lack of interest in God. For if we have no real interest in praising Him, it shows that we have never realized who He is. For when one becomes conscious of who God really is, and when one realizes that He who is Almighty, and infinitely Holy, has "done great things to us," the only possible reaction is the cry of half-articulate exultation that bursts from the depths of our being in amazement at the tremendous, inexplicable goodness of God to men. The Psalms are all made up of such cries—cries of wonder, exultation, anguish or joy. The very concreteness of their passion makes some of them seem disjointed and senseless. Their spontaneity makes them songs without plan, because there are no blueprints for ecstasy.

Yet at the same time, the Psalms are rugged and sober. Their emotions are controlled, and the very control increases their intensity. Add to this the even more plain sobriety with which the Church herself uses the Psalter, and we find that the tremendous impact of the Psalms is buried at a very deep spiritual level, and that we must pray on that level in order to feel it at all.

To say that the Psalms are deep is not to say that they are esoteric. One does not have to be a very unusual person in order to appreciate them. One has to be a healthy, simple person with a lot of faith and enough freedom from the tastes and prejudices of our time to be able to appreciate the imagery of another race and age. We must be, to some extent, "Orientals."

*   *   *

When we praise God, says St. Augustine, there must be order in our praise. It must be intelligent, spiritual. We must not be carried away by emotionalism. Nor should we on the other hand be so "objective" that there is no longer anything personal in our prayer to God. In order that we may remain on the straight road, turning neither to the right nor to the left, "the best way is to seek the way of praise in the Scriptures of God." *(Melius iter laudis in Scriptura Dei quaerimus.)*

St. Augustine adds that God has taught us to praise Him, in the Psalms, not in order that He may get something out of this praise, but in order *that we may be made better by it.* Praising God in the words of the Psalms, we can come to know Him better. Knowing Him better we love Him better, loving Him better we find our happiness in Him. "Therefore, because He knew that this would be for our benefit, He made Himself more lovable to us by praising Himself." These words, taken from St. Augustine's commentary on Psalm 144, are supplemented by others in his *De Doctrina Christiana,* where he says: "God wants to be loved not in order that He may get something out of it, but in order that those who love Him may receive an eternal reward. And this reward is God Himself, whom they love." (*De Doct. Christ.* i:29.)

The contemplation we learn from the Psalter is not mere "speculation." The Psalms are not abstract treatises on the divine nature. In them we learn to know God not by analyzing various concepts of His divinity, but by praising and loving Him. The Psalms being hymns of praise, they only reveal their full meaning to those who use them in order to praise God.

To understand the Psalms, we must experience the sentiments they express, in our own hearts. We must sing them to God and make our own all the meaning they contain.

Hence, St. Augustine concludes, our eternal life of praise must begin here on earth, in time. All our thoughts, our "meditation" in this life should center on the praise of God "because the eternal exultation of our future life will be the praise of God, and no one can be fitted for that future life who has not exercised himself in praise

in this present life." (Commentary on Psalm 148.)
"Let no day go by in which I do not bless Thee,"
adds St. Augustine. We must praise Him as much
in sorrow as in joy, because "If we do not cease
to praise Him, even though we may seem to be
faring badly in a day of sorrow, yet all will be
well for us even then in our God." (Commentary
on Psalm 144.)

Why is this? Because the Psalms not only
form our minds according to the mind of the
Church, not only direct our thoughts and affec-
tions to God, but they *establish us in God*, they
unite us to Him in Christ. But they do this only
if our hearts follow their thoughts and words back
into the inspired source from which they have
come to us. Therefore the sentiments of the
Psalmist, which are the thoughts and sentiments
of God Himself in His Church, must lead us into
the hidden sanctuary of God. Where our treasure
is, there will our hearts be also. The function of
the Psalms is to reveal to us God as the "treasure"
whom we love because He has first loved us, and
to hide us, heart and soul, in the depths of His
infinite Light. The Psalms, therefore, lead us to
contemplation.

No one can doubt that the Church considers the Psalms the ideal prayer for her clerics and religious. They form the largest part of the divine office. But the main purpose of this short essay is to remind the reader that the Psalter is also a perfect form of prayer for the layman.

It would be quite wrong to imagine that the prayer life of the Church is divided into two distinct halves, separated by a gap that is rarely bridged, as if the Psalter and the Missal were reserved for clerics and the rosary and other extraliturgical devotions were for the laity. The very fact that the rosary was originally referred to as the "Layman's psalter" reminds us that before the Middle Ages the lay people participated in the divine office with the clerics, and chanted the Psalms with them. Other devotions arose only when the layman no longer understood the Psalms.

Of course it is quite clear that the rosary is the easiest and most accessible form of family prayer. His Holiness Pope Pius XII has told the whole Church that the rosary is one of the most effective remedies for the evils of our time, and his encyclical *"Ingruentium malorum"* expressed the desire to see the recitation of the family rosary spread more and more. Yet there is no reason why in the families of those who have a deeper liturgical sense and a wider background, the Psalms should not also form a part of family prayer.

In an allocution to the priests of Rome in 1949, His Holiness indicated that family prayers should be led by the father of the family if possible. "Instructed and accustomed to venerate and love the Holy Sacrifice of the Mass, Catholic men will easily become men of prayer and will make their families sanctuaries of prayer. And that is absolutely necessary . . . Men who seriously apply themselves to penetrate the meaning and the import of the Sacrifice of the Mass cannot fail to revive in themselves the spirit of self-mastery, of mortification, of subordination of earthly things to heavenly and of absolute obedience to the will and the law of God." (March 29, 1949.)

The same Holy Father, in *Mediator Dei*, showed how the Psalms and the divine office make it possible for all Christians to attain to the close union with God which is the "ideal of the Christian life." The prayer life of the Church continues on earth the prayer life of the Incarnate Word. "In assuming human nature the Divine Word introduced into this earthly exile a hymn which is sung in heaven for all eternity. He unites Himself with the whole human race and with it sings this hymn of praise to God." When we are chanting the Psalms, or reciting them privately, then, "through His Spirit in us Christ entreats the Father." But the subjective fruit of this divine and universal prayer, the prayer of Christ in His Church, depends on how faithfully we make the sentiments of the Psalms our own. "When in prayer the voice repeats those hymns written under the inspiration of the Holy Ghost . . . it is necessary that the interior sentiment of our soul should accompany the voice so as to make those sentiments our own in which we are elevated to heaven."

In praying the Psalms, we make them "encompass the full round of the day and sanctify it." Uniting ourselves with Christ in His praying Church, we dedicate ourselves and all our actions to God in and through Him. For this, it is not necessary to take part in the public and official prayer of the Church. Used as private prayer, the Psalms unite us to the praying Church though in a less formal and official manner, because the Psalms are always the Church's prayer. Together with the Our Father, which Jesus Himself gave us, the Psalms are in the most perfect sense the "prayer of Christ." They not only contain the ancient promises which Christ Himself came to fulfill, but they show forth everywhere the glory of Jesus, His supreme and eternal power as King and Priest. Above all they show Him to us triumphant over death and over His enemies, who are also our own, and they promise us that He will return in triumph. As we recite the Psalms, His mysteries are actualized by grace in our own hearts and we participate in them with the whole Church. Therefore even in our private prayer Christ and the Church pray in us when we pray with the Holy Spirit. Nowhere can we be more certain that we are praying with the Holy Spirit than when we pray the Psalms.

Note also that Christ prays in us when we *meditate* on the Psalms, and does so perhaps even more perfectly than when we recite them vocally. For in proportion as we enter into the meaning of the Psalms, grace can better seize our minds and wills and unite them to the soul of the Divine Savior.

So therefore all that Pope Pius XII said above about the father of the family carrying over the spirit of the morning Mass into his family prayers will be most perfectly realized if he is able to make good use of the Psalms. A Catholic father or mother ought to know and appreciate the Psalms enough to be able to select one or another from among them which will most *perfectly suit the needs of the family* in any given situation, whether it be one of joy or sorrow, hope or trial, prosperity or failure. In all these, the family as a group ought to be able to articulate its sentiments and needs in the inspired work of the Scriptures, speaking to the Father in the person of His divine Son, moved and united and strengthened by the fire of the Holy Spirit.

I know of a Catholic layman, a teacher of Gregorian chant and a father of a large family, whose wife each night sang her children to sleep with a short responsory from the liturgy—and this without any "artiness" or artificiality at all. What could more perfectly fit the needs of a Catholic family than the thoughts and the moods of the Church herself, expressed in her prayers and in her chant? However, the special modality of family prayer demands that the universal sentiments of the liturgy and of the Psalms be *selected* and *applied* intelligently and lovingly to the concrete needs which are a matter of experience, perhaps of urgent experience, in the family at the time.

These same thoughts apply also to other groups—societies, clubs, Catholic Action units, seminaries, schools. One might also add that the starvation rations which go to make up the public prayers of some communities of religious sisters in the active life might profitably be strengthened by the addition of an occasional Psalm.

One might divide "men of prayer" into three groups, according to their attitudes towards the Psalms.

The first group admits in theory that the Psalms are a perfect form of prayer (otherwise the Church would not use them), but they are unable to use them in their own prayer and never in fact do so. If they are bound to say the Office, they say it without much appreciation or understanding.

The second group can be said to have a strong conviction of the value of the Psalms, and this conviction is a moving force in their lives. But it still does not permit them to *enter into* the Psalms. This is the case of some monks and clerics who are firmly, even belligerently, loyal to the supremacy of public vocal prayer over all other forms of prayer. When they take up the breviary, or go to choir, they are firmly convinced that they are doing a very important thing, and they go about it with a reverence and care proportionate to their conviction. But their zeal remains largely material and exterior. They do not know the meaning of the Psalms, and do not really care to know their meaning. It is sufficient for them that the Church should know what the Psalms mean. Their business is to recite them with meticulous care.

The third group, which is a small minority, consists of those who *know by experience* that the Psalms are a perfect prayer, a prayer in which Christ prays in the Christian soul uniting that soul to the Father in Himself. They have entered into the Psalms with faith. They have in a sense "lived" out the meaning of some of the Psalms in their own lives. They have tasted and seen that the Lord is sweet. Or, indeed, they have been privileged to share with Him the chalice of His Passion.

The only really practical question to be answered in the context of this essay is: how does one arrive at such an appreciation of the Psalms?

It is possible that a layman who does not recite the Office out of obligation may have an advantage over the cleric *in sacris* who is bound to the breviary. The fact that the Psalms become a habit is certainly of little value if they become a bad habit. And it is not a good habit to rush through the Psalms without any attention to their meaning, simply in order to fulfill an obligation as speedily as possible. Of course everyone is aware that it is practically unavoidable that a priest should sometimes say his Office in a hurry: he can hardly do otherwise, with the amount of work that he has to do. But that still does not make the rapid recitation of the Psalms a good habit. On the contrary, a conscientious cleric may come to the point when he has so few opportunities to pray his Office that he is fraught with tension and feelings of guilt and frustration which do not help his union with God. These constitute a special problem, with which I have no intention of dealing here.

One of the best ways to learn to appreciate the Psalms is to acquire a habit of reciting them slowly and well. And for this it is decidedly helpful to be able to limit one's recitation to just a few Psalms or to one only. To recite the Office slowly and meditatively is a luxury which will be rarely within the reach of a busy priest. But there is nothing to prevent a layman from taking just one Psalm a day, for instance in his night prayers, and reciting it thoughtfully, pausing to meditate on the lines which have the deepest meaning for him. A priest can achieve the same effect by making his morning meditation on a favorite Psalm.

Many people who would be capable of savoring the Psalms in this way without too much trouble, are held back by an inordinate fear that the Psalms may be too difficult to understand. They feel that one cannot begin to meditate on the Psalms unless one has first thoroughly studied them with a commentary. And commentaries go into such bewildering detail. But this fear is without foundation.

In our private, personal use of the Psalms, we need only have occasional recourse to a commentary to solve our major perplexities. In the ordinary course of events, a good modern translation of the Psalter is all we need. The recent Latin translation by the Biblical Institute, published in English by Benziger Brothers, has been edited as a prayer book with all the aids an educated Catholic will require to make the Psalms a real prayer. No further technical paraphernalia are necessary.

If anyone wants to know what a serious use of the Psalms involves, let him read Claudel's French version of the Psalms. The book is called *"Paul Claudel repond les Psaumes."* It is a book of Claudel's poems, in which the poet simply makes the themes of the Psalms his own, restating them in his own words. This is far from being a mere paraphrase. The Psalms have *entered into* the poet's whole life and being. They have become so much a part of him, that he is as it were a twentieth century psalmist, saying over again what David and the others said thousands of years ago. But the astonishing thing is that the poems come from the poet's heart *brand new.* Yet they lose nothing of their character, nothing of their identity. Psalm 46 *(Deus deorum Dominus locutus est)* is still definitely Psalm 46 in Claudel's

French. And yet it is a terrific new poem, a the-
ophany in which the nations gather around the
throne of God. There is nothing whatever archaic
about the poem. Its actuality, the actuality of the
divine Kingship, is overpoweringly real, even
though the language is still the language of kingship and thrones, and there are no longer on this
earth many kings and thrones: or at least few
kings whose thrones express power. Claudel's soul
has *answered* the Holy Spirit speaking in the ancient Psalm. Although one cannot decently com-
pare poetic inspiration with the inspiration of the
Scriptures, one is tempted to say that the Holy
Spirit has answered and echoed Himself in the
heart of this great religious poet.

Now, in order to keep clear, let us prescind
entirely from the whole question of mystical contemplation. Can we live the Psalms in this particular way without any special gift of God? Can
we come to appreciate and "experience" the inner meaning of the Psalms without departing from
the ordinary ways of prayer? Certainly we can.
All that we need is the ability to understand the
meaning of the Psalms, their literal meaning as
poems, and to "echo" or answer their meaning
in our own experience. Religious experience is
born of loving faith.

The experience that makes the Psalms a real,

deep, personal possession of our own hearts must be at the same time religious and poetic. Experiences which are essentially human and "natural" are transfigured by the theological virtues. Joy and sorrow, expectation and fear, anguish, desperation, triumph, peace: all these emotions have their part in our lives. They are also the material of the Psalms. The problem is therefore not to learn from the Psalms a totally new experience, but rather to recognize, in the Psalms, our own experience lived out and perfected, orientated to God and made fruitful, by the action of loving faith. Ultimately we do this by uniting our joys with the joys of Christ in the Psalms, our sorrows with the sorrows of Christ, and thus allowing ourselves to be carried to heaven on the tide of His victory.

*   *   *

If there is one theme that is certainly to be found implicitly or explicitly in all the Psalms, it is the *motif* of Psalm One: "Blessed is the man who follows not the counsel of the ungodly . . . but his delight is in the law of the Lord." If there is one "experience" to which the Psalms all lead in one way or another, it is precisely this: delight

in the law of the Lord, *peace in the will of God.*
This is the foundation on which the psalmists
build their edifice of praise.

Now there is not one of us who does not seek
peace. If the Psalms are sometimes anguished,
sometimes tormented, turbulent, warlike, defiant,
yet they all end in peace, or show us that the way
to peace is in confidence in the Strong Living God
who is far above the struggles and tempests of
earth, and who, nevertheless, descends on the
wings of the whirlwind to rescue His elect.

There is therefore one fundamental religious
experience which the Psalms can all teach us: *the
peace that comes from submission to God's will
and from perfect confidence in Him.*

This, then, gives us our guiding principle in
praying the Psalms. No matter whether we understand a Psalm at first or not, we should take
it up with this end in view: to make use of it as
a prayer that will *enable us to surrender ourselves
to God.* If we keep this one thing in mind, the
various Psalms will gradually yield their mysteries to us, and we will begin to find out that *certain ones fit our own condition and our own experience better than others.* This recognition of a special appropriateness for our own lives, in particular
Psalms, is an actual grace of God. It is an invita-
tion of the Holy Spirit, urging us to pay more at-

tention to these Psalms, to use them more
frequently in our prayers and meditations, to
adopt them for our own use. They become "our"
Psalms. We do not have to tell other people about
our preference, preach about it or write books
about it. We simply need to take possession of
these Psalms, "move in" to them, so to speak. Or
rather we move them into the house of our own
soul so that we think of our ordinary experiences
in their light and with their words.

There are some Psalms which calmly and
happily communicate the whole atmosphere of
a life of perfect submission to God. Take for instance Psalm 14, or 66, or 33.

> Behold, the unhappy man cried, and the Lord
> heard,
>> and rescued him from all his straits.
> The angel of the Lord encamps round them that
> fear him;
>> and he rescues them.
> Taste and see how good is the Lord;
>> blessed is the man who flees to him for refuge.
> Fear the Lord, O ye his saints,
>> for they that fear him know no want.
> The powerful have become poor and have
> hungered;
>> but they that seek the Lord shall lack no good
>> thing.

—*Psalm* 33:7-11

Above all, Psalm 118, the longest of them all, is a litany of praises extolling the peace that is found in the will of God. This Psalm, which might at first seem dull and "juridical"—since it praises the Torah from beginning to end—turns out, on long acquaintance, to be one of the most contemplative of them all. St. Ambrose, indeed, commented on it in terms appropriate to the *Canticle of Canticles.* It is a song of the soul that rejoices in perfect self-surrender to God.

Pointing out that in this Psalm 118, as well as in the various sapiential books, moral and mystical meanings are mingled together, St. Ambrose describes how the Church welcomes the coming of Christ in this Psalm:

> "Holy Church, who in the beginning of the world was espoused to God in paradise, who was prefigured in the deluge, announced by the Law, called by the prophets, has long awaited the redemption of men and the beauty of the Gospel. She now runs, impatient of delay, to kiss the Spouse, exclaiming: 'Let Him kiss me with the kiss of His mouth.'"
>
> *In Psalmum* CXVIII. MPL 15:1201

Chanting the numerous verses of this long hymn to the will of God, we learn to recognize, in God's will for us, the fulfilment of the Mystery of Christ in our own lives, and we hasten to cooperate with the action of the Holy Spirit, who, in all that He does, strives to unite the sons of the Church more closely in the unity of the Mystical Christ.

When we are fully and whole-heartedly united with the will of God and striving to bear one another's burdens and build the mystical City of God on this earth, we find our peace-filled hearts spontaneously overflowing with that praise of God which is the joy of the poor whom He has deigned to call to the riches of divine sonship. *Rectos decet collaudatio!* (Praise is fitting in those who are sincere with God.)

Other Psalms of luminous peace in the life of obedience are 15, 19, 24, 61, 111, 124, etc.

> I keep the Lord always in my sight;
>   since he is at my right hand,
>   I shall not be moved.
> Therefore my heart rejoices
>   and my soul is glad;
>   even my body will rest secure.
> *—Psalm* 15:8-9

> All the ways of the Lord are kindness and faithfulness
>   for them that keep his covenant and his laws.
> *—Psalm* 24:10

Only in God be at rest, O my soul,
   for my hope comes from him.
Only he is my rock and my salvation,
   my stronghold:
    I shall not be moved.
With God is my salvation and my glory,
   the rock of my strength:
   my refuge is in God.
O thou people, hope in him at all times;
   pour out your hearts before him:
   God is a refuge for us!

—Psalm 61:6-9

They that trust in the Lord are as Mount Sion,
   which is not moved, which endures forever.
Mountains surround Jerusalem:
   so the Lord surrounds his people,
   both now and forever.

—Psalm 124:1-2

*   *   *

Sometimes these Psalms of confidence and submission are more poignant. Like Psalm 39, they spring from a heart that has to trust and obey under severe trial. "I hoped, I hoped in the Lord, and He bent down to me and heard my cry. And He drew me out of the pit of destruction . . . and He put into my mouth a new canticle, a song to our God." And here again, the purest joy springs up like a clear flame in the verse which proclaims: "I delight to do Thy will, O my God, and Thy law is in the depths of my heart." This is a verse which the New Testament interprets spiritually in Hebrews 10:5f, seeing in it the obedience and submission of Christ to His Father. The delight we feel at glimpsing the deep meaning of these few lines must be taken as a call of grace to enter more deeply into union with the Savior, hidden within the Psalm. We must take this impulsion of grace and use it in our own lives, becoming ourselves more obedient, and recognizing at the same time that if we are able to do so it is only because of the merits of the obedience of Him whom we have met in the obscurity of faith while reciting these lines, or, better still, while meditating upon their content.

We should have a special love for the Gradual Psalms (119–133). Perhaps these short, joyful songs are the most beautiful in the whole Psalter. They are full of light and confidence. They bring God very close to us. They open our hearts to the secret action of His peace and to His silent grace. St. Augustine calls them the Psalms of our journey to the heavenly Jerusalem. Indeed, they are supposed to have been the favorite songs of pilgrims traveling to the earthly Jerusalem before the time of Christ. Hence their name "Gradual" Psalms for the "stages" (degrees-*gradus*) of the journey.

One of the most typical is Psalm 121:

I rejoiced, because they said to me:
   'We shall go into the house of the Lord.'
Our feet are already standing within thy gates,
   O Jerusalem,
Jerusalem, which is built as a city,
   all compact in itself.
Thither the tribes go up, the tribes of the Lord,
   according to the law of Israel,
   to praise the name of the Lord.
There are set thrones of judgment,
   the thrones of the house of David.
Pray ye for the things
   that are for the peace of Jerusalem!
   May they be safe that love thee!
Peace be within thy walls,
   safety in thy palaces!
For the sake of my brethren and my companions,
   I will say:
   Peace be within thee!
Because of the house of the Lord, our God,
   I will entreat good things for thee.

Many of the Psalms are most appropriate for times of suffering and trial. Our life in the society of fallen men is not always easy or smooth. There

are misunderstandings, conflicts, sometimes grave
injustices to be borne in silence. At such times,
our souls need strength and can seek it in such
Psalms as Psalm 12: "How long, O Lord, wilt thou
utterly forget me? How long wilt thou hide Thy
face from me?" Or Psalm 30: "For I have heard
the hissing of the crowd—terror is everywhere!
Assembling together against me, they planned to
take away my life." Here again, in our sufferings
and perils, we find ourselves united with the Mys-
terious Companion who looms up at our side, or
indeed within the depths of our soul, as we recite
the Psalms. It is Christ who has suffered before
us, and for us. He has come to us in the Psalm.
If we had not recited it, perhaps we would not
have found Him at all, and we might have gone
our own way into despair.

Particularly appropriate for suffering in-
justice and calumny are Psalms 25, 53, 55.

> Take not my soul away with sinners,
>   nor my life with murderers,
> In whose hands is crime,
>   and whose right hand is filled with bribes.
> But I walk in my innocence:
>   redeem me and have mercy on me.
> My foot stands in a level way;
>   in the assemblies I will bless the Lord.
>   —*Psalm* 25:9-12

The fool says in his heart: 'There is no God.'
They are corrupt,
    they have done things that must be abhorred;
    there is not one that does what is good.
God looks down from heaven upon the sons of
    men,
    to see if there be one who understands and
    seeks God.
All have gone astray together,
    they are turned to wickedness;
    there is not one that does what is right,
    there is not even one.
Will they not return to their senses, they that do
    evil,
    that eat up my people as they eat bread,
    that call not upon God?

                       —*Psalm* 52:2-5

O God, save me by thy name,
    and plead my cause by thy might.
O God, hear my prayer,
    give ear to the words of my mouth.
For proud men have risen against me,
    and violent men have sought my life;
    they have not set God before their eyes.

                       —*Psalm* 53:2-5

Psalm 27 is one of the most beautiful of all prayers
for help in affliction.

Unto thee I cry, O Lord;
   my rock, be not deaf to me,
Lest, if thou hear me not,
   I become like unto them
   that go down into the pit.
Hearken to the voice of my pleading,
   when I cry unto thee,
   when I lift up my hands to thy holy temple.
Drag me not away with sinners
   and with evildoers.

—*Psalm* 27:1-3

Other Psalms enter more deeply into the mystery of interior and spiritual trial. There is no night of the soul that has not been experienced before us by the psalmists, who, in their turn, were simply prefiguring the agony of Christ in the garden. Consider for instance Psalms 62, 38, 40, 31, 54, 58.

O God, thou art my God:
   earnestly I seek thee,
My soul thirsts for thee, my flesh longs for thee,
   like a dry and thirsty land, without water.

—*Psalm* 62:2

I was struck dumb, I am silent:
   For thou hast done it.
Remove thy scourge from me:
   I am consumed by the blow of thy hand.

—*Psalm* 38:10-11

Listen to me and hearken to me!
    I am driven hither and thither in my anguish.
And I am troubled because of the voice of the
        foe,
    and the cry of the sinner;
For they bring down evil upon me,
    and with anger they attack me.
My heart is troubled within me,
    and the terror of death falls upon me.
Fear and trembling are come upon me,
    and horror overwhelms me.
And I say: Oh, had I wings like a dove,
    I would fly away and be at rest.

—Psalm 54:3-7

As long as I was silent my bones wasted away
    amid my continual groanings.
For day and night thy hand was heavy upon me,
    my strength was burned up as by the heats of
        summer.

—Psalm 31:3-4

Then there is Psalm 41, in which the sufferings of the soul that thirsts for God are blended with mystical joy:

As the hind pants for the water brooks,
    so my soul pants after thee, O God.
My soul thirsts for God, for the living God:
    when shall I come and see the face of God?

My tears have become my bread day and night,
   whilst they say to me daily: Where is thy God?
                                    —*Psalm* 41:2-4

It is the joy of a soul that knows how to hope in
the hour that would otherwise seem nothing but
despair.

Besides our own personal trials, we find in
the Psalms the sufferings and struggles of society.
That is to say, the sufferings of that society of
souls chosen by Christ and united to Him in one
Body—the sufferings and struggles of the Church.
These perhaps are the Psalms that apply most to
the world of our time. Take for instance the Second Psalm:

Why are the nations in tumult,
   and why do the peoples devise vain things?
The kings of the earth rise up,
   and the princes take counsel together
   against the Lord and against his
      Anointed: . . . .
He who dwells in the heavens laughs,
   the Lord laughs them to scorn.
                                    —*Psalm* 2:1-2, 4

Here too we can use Psalms 9, 11, 13, 5, 52, 49,
51, 29, 82, 107. All these are deeply moving if we
use them as prayers for peace and help in times
of persecution like our own.

The greatest of evils is sin. And there are many Psalms, particularly the penitential Psalms (6, 31, 37, 50, 101, 129, 142), which express heart-broken sorrow for having offended God.

> Rebuke me not, O Lord, in thy wrath,
>   nor chastise me in thy fury.
> For thy arrows are fastened in me,
>   and thy hand has fallen upon me.
> There is no health in my body
>   because of thy indignation,
> There is no soundness in my bones
>   because of my sin.
>
> —*Psalm* 37:2-4

> Turn thy face away from my sins,
>   and blot out all my iniquities.
> Create a pure heart for me, O God,
>   and renew in me a steadfast spirit.
> Cast me not away from thy face,
>   and take not thy holy spirit from me.
> Restore unto me the joy of thy salvation,
>   and strengthen me with a noble spirit.
>
> —*Psalm* 50:11-14

The penitential Psalms are of course often used as prayers for the dead, especially 129, the *De Profundis*, which all Catholics should know by heart.

Out of the depths I cry unto thee, O Lord,
    Lord, hear my voice!
Let thine ears become attentive
    to the voice of my supplication.
If thou, O Lord, keep the memory of offenses,
    Lord, who shall stand?
But with thee there is forgiveness of sins,
    so that thou art served with reverential fear.
I hope in the Lord,
    my soul hopes in his word;
My soul longs for the Lord,
    more than watchmen for the dawn.
More than watchmen for the dawn,
    Israel longs for the Lord,
Because with the Lord there is mercy
    and with him plentiful redemption:
And he shall redeem Israel
    from all her iniquities.

—*Psalm* 129

Turning from sorrow to joy, we find that the most joyful Psalms, and the most admirable of them all, are the great Psalms of praise and adoration of God. These are what one might call the Psalms *par excellence.* They are more truly Psalms than all the others, for the real purpose of a Psalm is to praise God. The reason why we submit entirely to His will is because He is good. We do not obey merely for the sake of obedience, but as a testimony to the supreme goodness of God

Himself. We are happy to serve Him not only because He gives us good things, but also because praising His goodness is itself our highest joy.

> Give thanks to the Lord, for he is good;
> > for his mercy endures forever.
> > > —*Psalm* 117:1

> Praise ye the Lord, for he is good,
> > sing ye to our God, for he is sweet:
> > praise is becoming to him.
> > > —*Psalm* 146:1

> I will extol thee, O my God, O king;
> > and I will bless thy name for ever and ever.
> Every day I will bless thee,
> > and I will praise thy name for ever and ever.
> > > —*Psalm* 144:1-2

> Praise the Lord, O my soul;
> > in my life I will praise the Lord;
> > I will sing to my God as long as I shall be.
> > > —*Psalm* 145:2

Joy in praising God is the pure essence of the spirit of the Church's prayer, and it is the reward of a soul that knows how to penetrate fully by faith, love and perfect submission to God, into the deepest meaning of the Psalter.

When we have thus entered perfectly into the life of praise that the Psalms hold in store for us, then the Lord becomes our joy, (Psalms 15, 22, 32, 33). He is our light (Psalms 26, 118, 122, etc.) and our strength (45, 141, 124, etc.).

The Lord is my shepherd: I want for nothing;
    he makes me to lie in green pastures,
He leads me to waters where I may rest;
    he restores my soul.

—Psalm 22:1-2

Our soul waits for the Lord:
    he is our helper and our shield;
Therefore in him our heart rejoices,
    in his holy name we trust.
Let thy mercy, O Lord, be upon us,
    according as we hope in thee!

—Psalm 32:20-22

Blessed be the Lord, my Rock,
    who teaches my hands battle,
    my fingers war,
My mercy and my stronghold,
    my defense and my deliverer,
My shield and my refuge,
    who subjects the peoples to me.

—Psalm 143:1-2

No doubt the finest and most moving of all the Psalms, for a Christian, are those clearly Messianic poems in which the sufferings and triumph of Christ are brought before the eyes of our soul with an incomparable vividness. What more powerful prayer would there be than Psalm 21, in which we unite ourselves with the dying Savior on the Cross, bury our sorrows in His pierced Heart, and feel our sins washed away by the saving tide of His Most Precious Blood—

> They open their mouth against me,
>> like a lion ravening and roaring.
>
> I am poured out like water,
>> and all my bones are disjointed:
>
> My heart has become like wax,
>> it melts in my bowels.
>
> My throat is dried up like a potsherd,
>> and my tongue cleaves to my jaws;
>> thou hast brought me down
>> to the dust of death.
>
> For many dogs beset me,
>> a band of evildoers prowls around me.
>
> They have dug my hands and my feet,
>> I can number all my bones.
>
> But they watch me,
>> and seeing me, they rejoice;
>> they divide my garments among them,
>> and for my tunic they cast lots.
>
> —*Psalm* 21:14-19

Then again we can turn to the triumphant Christ, victorious over death and seated at the right hand of God in Psalm 109, one of the most important Psalms in the liturgy of the Church.

> The Lord said to my Lord:
>> 'Sit thou at my right hand,
>> until I make thy enemies thy footstool.'
> The Lord will stretch forth
>> the scepter of thy power out of Sion:
>> Rule thou in the midst of thy foes!
> With thee is sovereignty on the day of thy birth
>> in the radiance of holiness:
>> like dew, before the day star, I begot thee.
>> —*Psalm* 109:1-3

Finally, the great eschatological Psalms, short, powerful and clear, open our eyes to the future, and fill our hearts with the sober and awe-struck joy which the Church feels as she contemplates the second coming of Christ (Psalms 95–99).

> Let the heavens be glad, and let the earth rejoice;
>> let the sea roar and the fulness thereof;
>> let the field exult and all that is therein.
> Then all the trees of the forest shall be joyful
>> before the Lord, for he comes,
>> for he comes to rule the earth.
> He will rule the world with justice,
>> and the peoples with his truth.
>> —*Psalm* 95:11-13

The Lord reigns: the people tremble;
    he sits above the Cherubim: the earth is
        moved.
The Lord is great in Sion
    and high above all the peoples.
Let them praise thy great and terrible name:
    it is holy.
And the mighty one reigns who loves justice:
    thou hast established the things that are right,
    thou dost justice and right in Jacob.
Extol ye the Lord our God,
    and fall down before his footstool: it is holy.
                                            —*Psalm* 98:1-5

There is no aspect of the interior life, no kind of
religious experience, no spiritual need of man that
is not depicted and lived out in the Psalms. But
we cannot lay hands on these riches unless we are
willing to work for them. The work to be done
has been suggested above. It is no longer so much
a matter of study, since the study has been done
for us by experts. We need only to take advantage of the texts they have given us, and use them
with faith, and confidence and love. Above all
we need zeal and strength and perseverance. We
cannot by mere human ingenuity or talent exhaust
all that is contained in the Psalms. Indeed, if we
seek only to "get something out of them" we will
perhaps get less than we expect, and generous ef-

forts may be frustrated because they are turned in the wrong direction: toward ourselves rather than toward God.

In the last analysis, it is not so much what we get out of the Psalms that rewards us, as what we put into them. If we really make them our prayer, really prefer them to other methods and expedients, in order to let God pray in us in His own words, and if we sincerely desire above all to offer Him this particularly pure homage of our Christian faith, then indeed we will enter into the meaning of the Psalms, and they will become our favorite vocal prayers.

The Sanctity of the Most Holy Mother of God, who is our model as well as our most powerful Protector in the life of Grace, was nourished and increased by her love for these inspired texts. Mary understood the Psalms as no one else could understand them: she meditated on them constantly, keeping all their words and pondering them in her Heart. Her *Magnificat* sprang from the depths of her soul and gives us a kind of synthesis and summary of all the poetry of the Old Testament. With her as our guide and teacher, we will easily come to love the Psalms and to appreciate their hidden beauty.

In this way, our life of prayer will come to reproduce something of the inner life of the Holy Mother of God.